How to draw
ANIMALS

Hello!

Thank you very much for choosing my book:
How to Draw Animals For Kids

I sincerely hope that you find it entertaining and helpful. I would like to hear from you if you could take some time to post a review on Amazon!

Your feedback and comments will help us improve for future books and make this book even better.

Thank you
Eva Harlow

WELCOME!

THIS BOOK BELONGS TO

TIPS FOR USING THIS BOOK

1- Have your materials ready!
A pencil, an eraser, colored pencils or crayons

2- Follow the step-by-step instructions and
   numbers to draw these cute animals

3- Draw loosely and slowly with light lines

4- Darken the lines and add your own details!

5- Keep practicing and enjoy, practice
   makes perfect!

CONTENT

ELEPHANT	OWL	SNAIL	BEE	FISH
			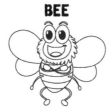	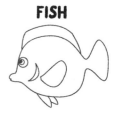

TOUCAN	SQUIRREL	CHAMELEON	PARROT	DOG

CHICKEN	DOLPHIN	TORTOISE	SEAHORSE	MONKEY

HAMSTER	COW	BUTTERFLY	FOX	CAT

FROG	HUMMINGBIRD	PANDA	LLAMA	MOUSE

GOAT	SHARK	LION	ZEBRA	OCTOPUS	PENGUIN

ELEPHANT

1

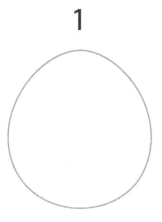

2

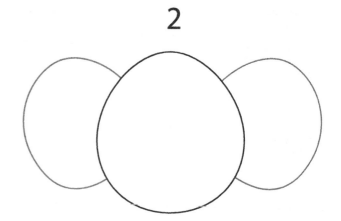

3

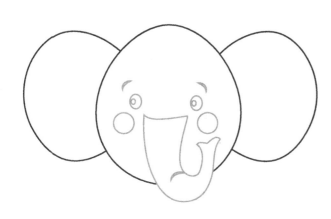

4

5

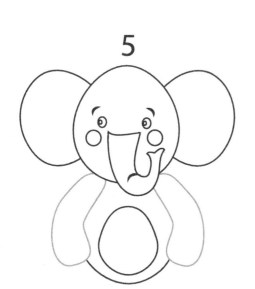

6

DID YOU KNOW?
Elephants communicate
through vibrations

Let's trace and practice!

Draw your elephant here!

OWL

1

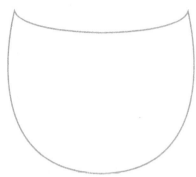

2

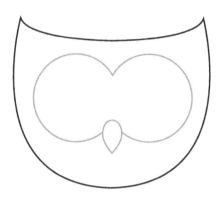

3

4

5

6

DID YOU KNOW?
Owls can turn their heads
almost completely around

Let's trace and practice!

Draw your owl here!

SNAIL

1

2

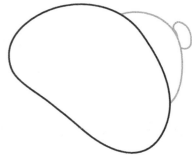

3

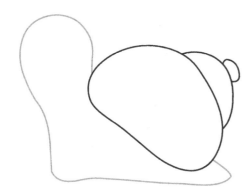

4

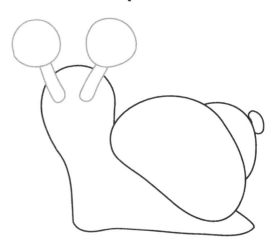

5

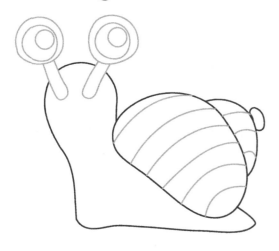

Draw your elephant here

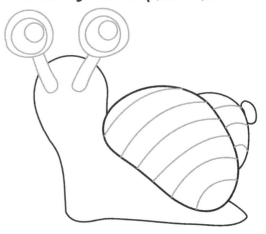

Let's trace and practice!

Draw your snail here!

BEE

1

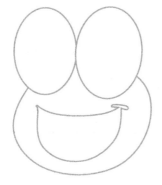

2

3

4

5

6

DID YOU KNOW?
Bees live in hives with 3 types of
members: Queen, Workers, Drones

Let's trace and practice!

Draw your bee here!

FISH

1

2

3

4

5

DID YOU KNOW?
fish breathe through
their gills

Let's trace and practice!

Draw your fish here!

TOUCAN

1

2

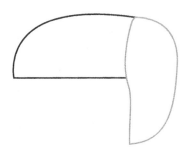

3

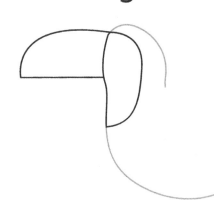

4

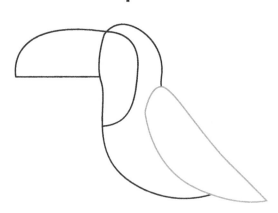

5

6

DID YOU KNOW?
Toucans are frugivorous, meaning
they are fruit-eating creatures

Let's trace and practice!

Draw your toucan here!

SQUIRREL

1

2

3

4

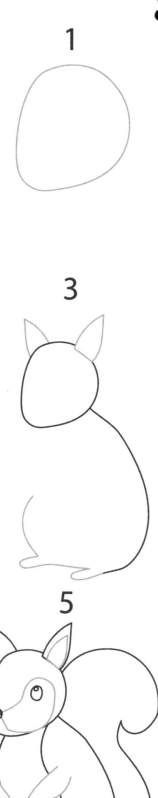

5

6

Let's trace and practice!

Draw your squirrel here!

CHAMELEON

1

2

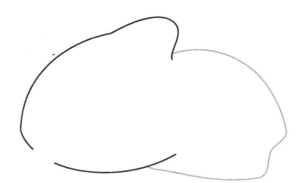

3

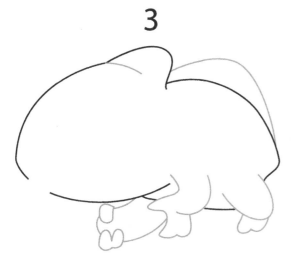

4

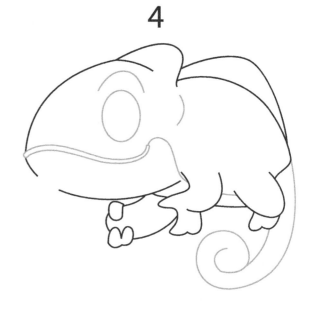

5

6

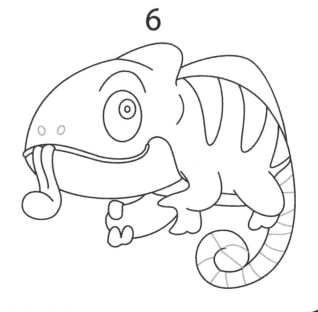

DID YOU KNOW?
Chameleons live in bushes
and trees and not on the ground

Let's trace and practice!

Draw your chamaleon here!

PARROT

1

2

3

4

5

6

DID YOU KNOW?
Parrots can live up to
80 years old

Let's trace and practice!

Draw your parrot here!

DOG

1

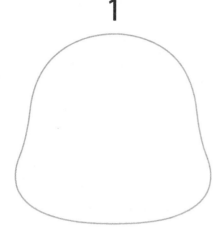

2

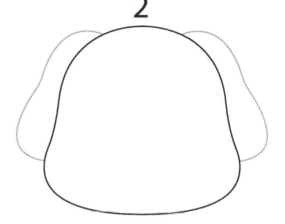

3

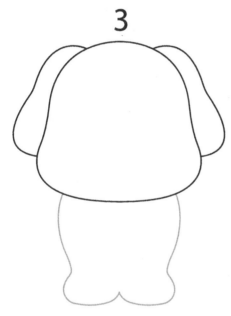

4

5

6

Let's trace and practice!

Draw your dog here!

CHICKEN

1

2

3

4

5

6

DID YOU KNOW?
Chickens are living
descendants of dinosaurs

Let's trace and practice!

Draw your chicken here!

DOLPHIN

1

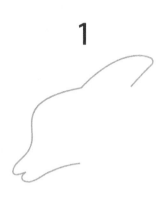

2

3

4

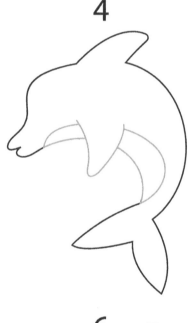

5

6

Let's trace and practice!

Draw your dolphin here!

TORTOISE

1

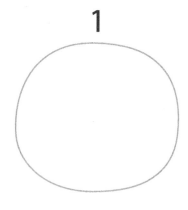

2

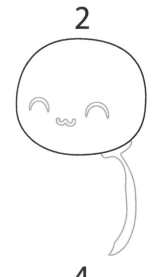

3

4

5

6

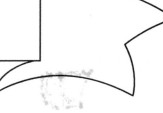

DID YOU KNOW?
Tortoises smell with
their throats

Let's trace and practice!

Draw your tortoise here!

SEAHORSE

1

2

3

4

5

6

DID YOU KNOW?
Seahorses have necks, which
most fish do not

Let's trace and practice!

Draw your seahorse here!

MONKEY

1

2

3

4

5

6

DID YOU KNOW?
Monkeys sleep while sitting
in trees, often upright

Let's trace and practice!

Draw your monkey here!

HAMSTER

1

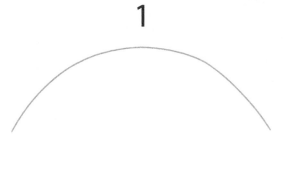

2

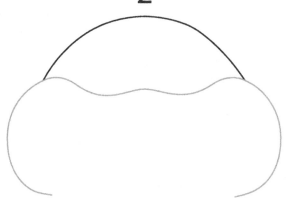

3

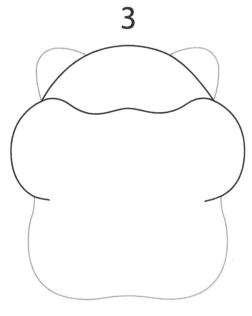

4

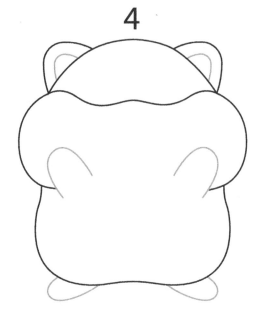

5

6

DID YOU KNOW?
Hamsters rely on scent to
find their way

Let's trace and practice!

Draw your hamster here!

COW

Let's trace and practice!

Draw your cow here!

BUTTERFLY

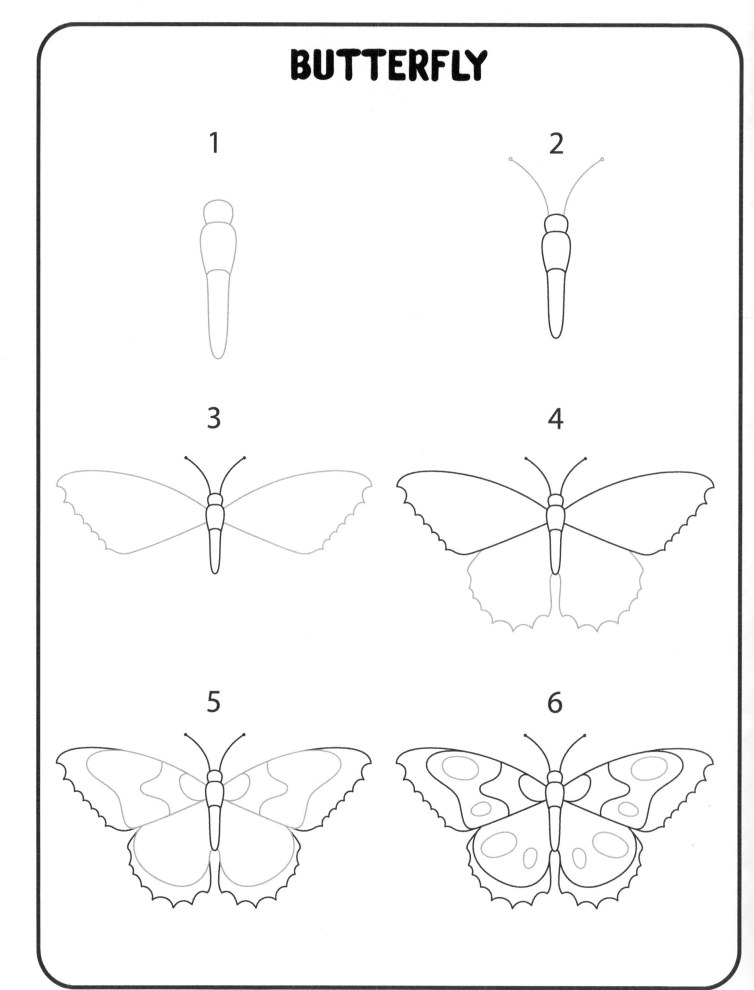

DID YOU KNOW?
Butterflies have taste buds
on their feet

Let's trace and practice!

Draw your buttetfly here!

FOX

1

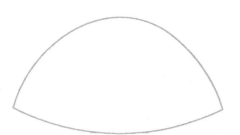

2

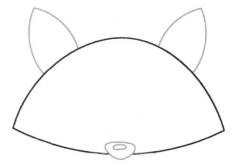

3

4

5

6

Let's trace and practice!

Draw your fox here!

CAT

1

2

3

4

5

6

DID YOU KNOW?
Cats can jump up to 6
times their height

Let's trace and practice!

Draw your cat here!

FROG

1

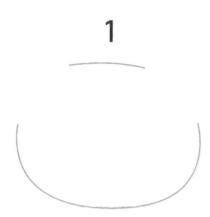

2

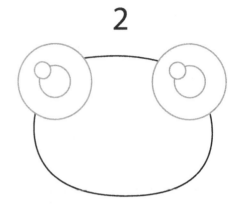

3

4

5

6

DID YOU KNOW?
Frogs have excellent night vision
and are sensitive to movement

Let's trace and practice!

Draw your frog here!

HUMMINGBIRD

DID YOU KNOW?
Hummingbirds are the only birds
that can fly backwards

Let's trace and practice!

Draw your hummingbird here!

PANDA

1

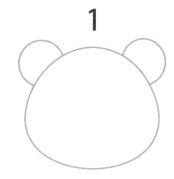

2

3

4

5

6

Let's trace and practice!

Draw your panda here!

LLAMA

1

2

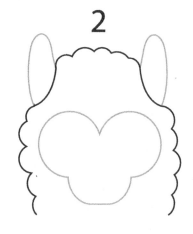

3

4

5

6

DID YOU KNOW?
Llamas do not have hair instead
they are covered in wool

Let's trace and practice!

Draw your llama here!

MOUSE

1

2

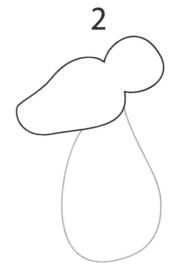

3

4

Let's trace and practice!

Draw your mouse here!

GOAT

1

2

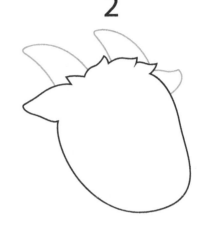

3

4

5

6

Let's trace and practice!

Draw your goat here!

SHARK

1

2

3

4

5

6

DID YOU KNOW?
Shark skin feels like sandpaper

Let's trace and practice!

Draw your shark here!

LION

1

2

3

4

5

6

Let's trace and practice!

Draw your lion here!

ZEBRA

1

2

3

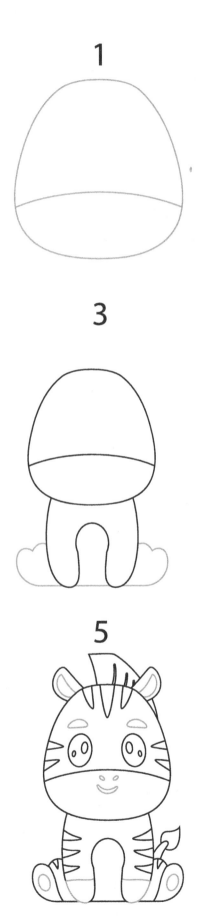

4

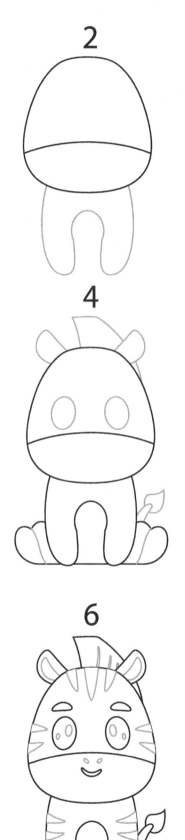

5

6

Let's trace and practice!

Draw your zebra here!

OCTOPUS

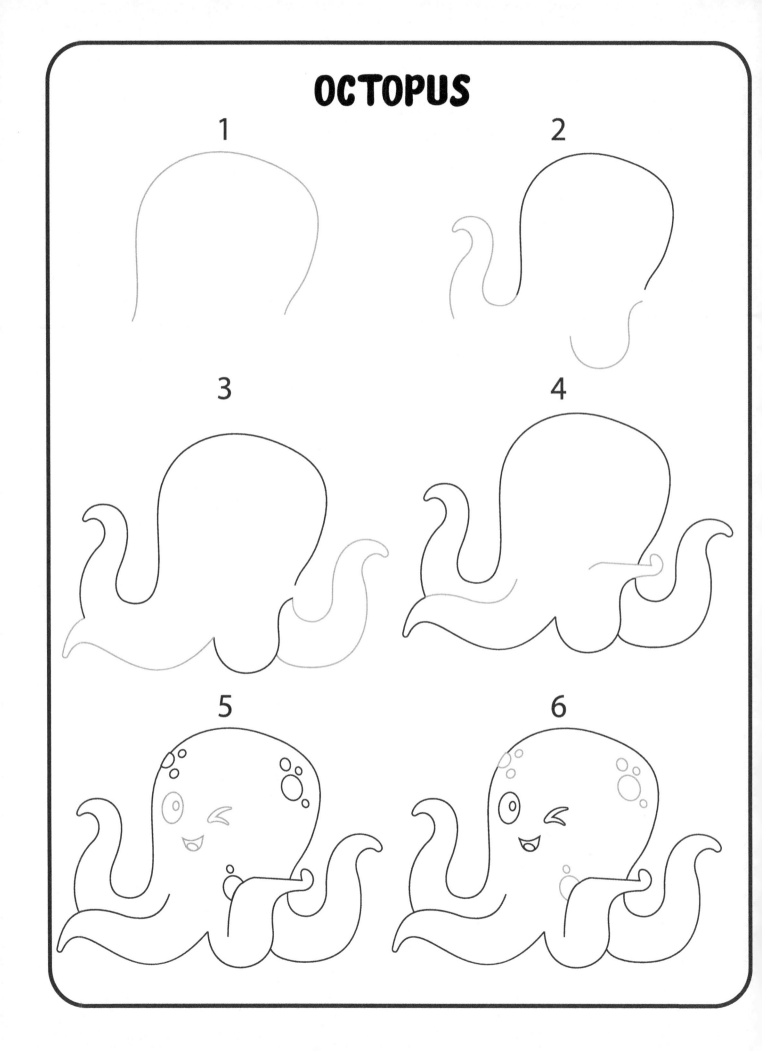

DID YOU KNOW?
Octopuses live alone in dens
made from rocks

Let's trace and practice!

Draw your octopus here!

PENGUIN

1

2

3

4

5

6

DID
Penguins they ... rs
instead of wings

Let's trace and practice!

Draw your penguin here!

Made in the USA
Las Vegas, NV
09 January 2023

65304770R00037